DOVER·THRIFT·EDITIONS

The Seven Against Thebes

AESCHYLUS

DOVER PUBLICATIONS, INC.
Mineola, New York

DOVER THRIFT EDITIONS

GENERAL EDITOR: PAUL NEGRI
EDITOR OF THIS VOLUME: JULIE NORD

Copyright

Published in Canada by General Publishing Company, Ltd., 30 Lesmill Road, Don Mills, Toronto, Ontario.

Theatrical Rights

Bibliographical Note

This Dover edition, first published in 2000, is an unabridged republication of *The Seven Against Thebes* from *The Suppliant Maidens, The Persians, The Seven Against Thebes, The Prometheus Bound of Aeschylus* translated into English verse by E. D. A. Morshead, originally published by Macmillan and Co., Ltd., London, in 1928. An introductory Note and several footnotes identifying persons and deities referred to by name in the play have been specially prepared for this edition.

Library of Congress Cataloging-in-Publication Data

Aeschylus.
   [Seven against Thebes. English]
   The seven against Thebes / Aeschylus.
      p. cm.
   Translated into English verse by E.D.A. Morshead.
   ISBN 0-486-41420-5
    1. Seven against Thebes (Greek mythology)—Drama. I. Morshead, E. D. A. (Edmund Doidge Anderson) II. Title.

PA3827.S4 M67 2000
882'.01—dc21

00-031389

Note

If anyone may be said to have "invented" the kind of drama we know as Greek tragedy, it was Aeschylus (525–455/6 B.C.). The drama he wrote, like that of his predecessors, was derived from choral song and dance, and played an important role in the religious and cultural life of the community. Traditionally, the players in each scene consisted of the chorus and a single actor; Aeschylus' stroke of genius was to add a second actor, thereby vastly increasing his works' dramatic possibilities.

The generation that followed Aeschylus brought the great dramatists Sophocles and Euripides, who added further refinements to the art form. With the surviving plays of these three—and there are only 32 such plays—we have all the complete examples left to us of one of the greatest and most influential arts of Western civilization. It is believed that Aeschylus himself wrote between seventy and one hundred plays in the 69 years of his life, of which just seven have come down to us. *The Seven Against Thebes* was the third play in a trilogy dramatizing the legend of Laius, whose defiance of the oracle at Delphi led to his own son Oedipus committing patricide (see Argument, page xi), and to tragedy for all his progeny. The two previous plays in this trilogy are no longer with us, but we do know that the trilogy as a whole won the dramatic crown in 467 B.C.

Much has been written about the fact that the name "Thebes" is never mentioned in this play. Instead the setting is referred to as "Cadmea" and the chorus as the "Cadmean maidens." It has been suggested that "Thebes" was not the name in use in Aeschylus' day and that, moreover, its unique appearance in the title only supports the belief that this title was created at a later date and has been retained simply by convention. In any case, Aeschylus' nomenclature serves to remind us that all the players in the drama are descendants of Cadmus, who seems to have unwittingly set the tone of violence and infighting that is played out in this story. The history of the city begins with Cadmus slaying a serpent sent by Ares, the god of war, to guard the area. Cadmus took the teeth of this serpent and scattered them across the ground; out of them grew a race of armed men who immediately began to fight one another. Those who survived became the first Cadmeans. Cadmea, then, was founded in a war-like spirit and in *The Seven Against Thebes* that spirit has continued to drive its people, producing tragedy after tragedy. Indeed, the rhetorician Gorgias (c. 483–376 B.C.) describes this work as "a drama brimming with Ares [the spirit of war]." This inexorable passing on of strife and violence in families—both those who are families by blood and those who are families in a civic sense—is one of the most timeless and profound themes of this work and of many other Greek dramas.

The action of *The Seven Against Thebes* is simplicity itself, but so designed as to lay bare for modern readers the religious, ceremonial nature of what Aeschylus had prepared for his audience. At the play's opening, Eteocles announces that the army of Argos is gathered outside the city gates and is preparing itself to attack. Although it is not stressed—surely Aeschylus restrains himself on this point to heighten the suspense as we wait for Polynices' name to come up—we know that Eteocles' own brother Polynices, who wants to win control of Cadmea back for himself, is the instigator of this campaign. A spy arrives and launches into what amounts to a litany: a careful, slowly-paced naming of each of the seven champions who lead this attack. For each champion, the spy gives a name, his nearest relation, a physical description, a listing of his particular strengths and the deeds for which he is famous (or infamous), the arms he carries and how they are decorated and the deity with whom each is associated— for most are regarded as being in favor with a certain god or goddess and therefore to be specially aided and protected by that being. The spy names as well the gate which each stands ready to storm, and sometimes repeats the words of the warrior as he readies himself to fight.

Eteocles answers each one of these reports point for point, naming the Cadmean champion who will be sent to defend the gate, describing *his* strengths and legendary deeds, and, in addition, commenting on the qualities of the Argives in such a way as to discount them and lessen their fearsomeness. After his response the chorus raises a prayer in support of his assertions which serves to express both their hope that Eteocles' reassurances will turn out to be justified and their fears lest he be wrong.

As the playwright works deliberately through each of the seven intimidating opponents in this way, we clearly see a form of communal prayer enacted. And the process is given special pathos because of the fact that the chorus is not simply townspeople or elders, but is entirely young, unmarried women. These are the Cadmeans who stand in the very most vulnerable position during the Argive attack. For one thing, should the Argive army succeed and take over their city, all these young women would almost certainly be taken as slaves and probably many would end up as rape victims. For another, the young Cadmean men lost in the fight are particularly precious to these women—among them may be the women's future husbands. The regular voicing of this particular group's desperation, fear and pleading throughout the drama keeps us in close touch with the magnitude of what's at stake in this battle.

Aeschylus relies heavily on allusion to deities, and family connections—allusions which would have had rich and complex meaning for his audience, but which can be hard for today's readers to puzzle out. The many deities mentioned should be widely familiar to us, although each may be referred to by all manner of regional names or by the mere mention of some special trait or other. What may bear comment is how integral these beings are to all aspects of Greek life, as revealed in this play. For it seems as we read that there is no person or place in which a god does not take a special interest. Every hero, every gate, every river, every city seems to have a supernatural protector—sometimes more than one! So all the conflcts played out are simultaneously human and divine. And it is clear, in the depiction of Argive blasphemies juxtaposed with the Cadmean effort at greater piety and humility, that no good outcome will be achieved without help from on high.

The family connections mentioned in the drama are as follows: Hyperbius is the son of Oenops, Amphiaraus the son of Oecleus, Tydeus the son of Oeneus, Melanippus the son of Astacus, Actor the son of Oenops (which makes him Hyperbius' brother), Megareus the son of Creon, and Parthenopaeus the son of Zeus and Atalanta. Note also that since Creon is Eteocles' and Polynices' uncle, his son Megareus is their cousin. All of these names would probably have been legendary to Aeschylus' audience, but even for 21st-century audiences they can carry great significance: they remind us that every warrior going into this battle is a member of someone's family and each one of them will be greatly mourned should he fall in battle. Thus the fate of one soldier is also the fate of an entire family; the struggle between two brothers, Eteocles and Polynices, and their looming tragedy, become the struggle and tragedy of all the families that make up their people. All of Cadmea and Argos stands poised to share and powerfully amplify their sad end.

Finally, in this litany each one of the seven gates is identified for its special history and associations. By the time we finish, it seems clear that all parties and places involved in the coming siege are precious both to gods, and to men and women, and that *all* are in peril. And the greatest of these perils is revealed in the news, which Aeschylus reserves for last, that at the seventh gate Eteocles will meet his own brother in man-to-man combat. The outcome of this ultimate conflict is, of course, tragedy.

The Seven Against Thebes

Argument

LAïus, king of the Cadmeans, was warned by the oracle of Delphi that he should not beget a child. But he disobeyed this command, and when a son was born to him, he cast the child away, that he might perish on Cithaeron. But a herdsman found the babe yet alive, and he was nourished in Corinth and grew to manhood, not knowing his true parentage, and was named Oedipus; and he slew, unknowingly, his father, Laius, and afterwards saved the town of the Cadmeans from a devouring monster, and married the widowed queen, Iocaste, and begat sons and daughters. But when he learned what he had wrought unwittingly, he fell into despair, and the queen slew herself. But before Oedipus died, he laid a curse upon his male children, Eteocles and Polynices, that they should make even division of the kingdom by the sword; and it fell out even so, for the two brothers strove together for the inheritance, and Polynices brought an army, from Argos, against Eteocles; and the brothers fought, and fell each by the other's hand, and the curse was fulfilled.

Dramatis Personæ

Eteocles, *son of Oedipus, ruler of Thebes*.

A Spy.

Chorus of Cadmean Maidens.

Antigone
Ismene } daughters of Oedipus, sisters of Eteocles.

A Herald.

The Seven Against Thebes

Scene—The Acropolis of Thebes.

[*Enter* ETEOCLES.]

ETEOCLES

    Clansmen of Cadmus, at the signal given
By time and season must the ruler speak
Who sets the course and steers the ship of State
With hand upon the tiller, and with eye
Watchful against the treachery of sleep.
For if all go aright, "thank Heaven," men say,
But if adversely—which may God forefend!—
One name on many lips, from street to street,
Would bear the bruit and rumour of the time,
"Down with Eteocles!"—a clamorous curse,
A dirge of ruin. May averting Zeus
Make good his title here, in Cadmus' hold!
You it beseems now—boys unripened yet
To lusty manhood, men gone past the prime
And increase of the full begetting seed,
And those whom youth and manhood well combined
Array for action—all to rise in aid
Of city, shrines, and altars of all powers
Who guard our land; that ne'er, to end of time,
Be blotted out the sacred service due
To our sweet mother-land and to her brood.
For she it was who to their guest-right called
Your waxing youth, was patient of the toil,
And cherished you on the land's gracious lap,

1

Alike to plant the hearth and bear the shield
In loyal service, for an hour like this.
Mark now! until to-day, luck rules our scale;
For we, though long beleaguered, in the main
Have with our sallies struck the foemen hard.
But now the seer, the feeder of the birds,
(Whose art unerring and prophetic skill
Of ear and mind divines their utterance
Without the lore of fire interpreted)
Foretelleth, by the mastery of his art,
That now an onset of Achaea's host
Is by a council of the night designed
To fall in double strength upon our walls.
Up and away, then, to the battlements,
The gates, the bulwarks! don your panoplies,
Array you at the breast-work, take your stand
On floorings of the towers, and with good heart
Stand firm for sudden sallies at the gates,
Nor hold too heinous a respect for hordes
Sent on you from afar: some god will guard!
I too, for shrewd espial of their camp,
Have sent forth scouts, and confidence is mine
They will not fail nor tremble at their task,
And, with their news, I fear no foeman's guile.

[*Enter* A Spy.]

THE SPY

Eteocles, high king of Cadmus' folk,
I stand here with news certified and sure
From Argos' camp, things by myself descried.
Seven warriors yonder, doughty chiefs of might,
Into the crimsoned concave of a shield
Have shed a bull's blood, and, with hands immersed
Into the gore of sacrifice, have sworn
By Ares, lord of fight, and by thy name,
Blood-lapping Terror, "Let our oath be heard—
Either to raze the walls, make void the hold
Of Cadmus—strive his children as they may—

Or, dying here, to make the foemen's land
With blood impasted." Then, as memory's gift
Unto their parents at the far-off home,
Chaplets they hung upon Adrastus' car,[1]
With eyes tear-dropping, but no word of moan.
For their steeled spirit glowed with high resolve,
As lions pant, with battle in their eyes.
For them, no weak alarm delays the clear
Issues of death or life! I parted thence
Even as they cast the lots, how each should lead,
Against which gate, his serried company.
Rank then thy bravest, with what speed thou may'st,
Hard by the gates, to dash on them, for now,
Full-armed, the onward ranks of Argos come!
The dust whirls up, and from their panting steeds
White foamy flakes like snow bedew the plain.
Thou therefore, chieftain! like a steersman skilled,
Enshield the city's bulwarks, ere the blast
Of war comes darting on them! hark, the roar
Of the great landstorm with its waves of men!
Take Fortune by the forelock! for the rest,
By yonder dawn-light will I scan the field
Clear and aright, and surety of my word
Shall keep thee scatheless of the coming storm.

ETEOCLES

O Zeus and Earth and city-guarding gods,
And thou, my father's Curse, of baneful might,
Spare ye at least this town, nor root it up,
By violence of the foemen, stock and stem!
For here, from home and hearth, rings Hellas' tongue.
Forbid that e'er the yoke of slavery
Should bow this land of freedom, Cadmus' hold!
Be ye her help! your cause I plead with mine—
A city saved doth honour to her gods!

[*Exit* ETEOCLES, *etc. Enter the* CHORUS OF MAIDENS.]

[1]Adrustus, father-in-law to Polynices, was king of Argos and the seven against
 Thebes were therefore under his command.

CHORUS

I wail in the stress of my terror, and shrill is my cry of despair.

The foemen roll forth from their camp as a billow, and onward they bear!

Their horsemen are swift in the forefront, the dust rises up to the sky,

A signal, though speechless, of doom, a herald more clear than a cry!

Hoof-trampled, the land of my love bears onward the din to mine ears.

As a torrent descending a mountain, it thunders and echoes and nears!

The doom is unloosened and cometh! O kings and O queens of high Heaven,

Prevail that it fall not upon us! the sign for their onset is given—

They stream to the walls from without, white-shielded and keen for the fray.

They storm to the citadel gates—what god or what goddess can stay

The rush of their feet? to what shrine shall I bow me in terror and pray?

O gods high-thronèd in bliss, we must crouch at the shrines in your home!

Not here must we tarry and wail: shield clashes on shield as they come—

And now, even now is the hour for the robes and the chaplets of prayer!

Mine eyes feel the flash of the sword, the clang is instinct with the spear!

Is thy hand set against us, O Ares, in ruin and wrath to o'erwhelm

Thine own immemorial land, O god of the golden helm?

Look down upon us, we beseech thee, on the land that thou lovest of old,

And ye, O protecting gods, in pity your people behold!

Yea, save us, the maidenly troop, from the doom and despair of the slave,

For the crests of the foemen come onward, their rush is
the rush of a wave
Rolled on by the war-god's breath! almighty one, hear us
and save
From the grasp of the Argives' might! to the ramparts of
Cadmus they crowd,
And, clenched in the teeth of the steeds, the bits clink hor-
ror aloud!
And seven high chieftains of war, with spear and with
panoply bold,
Are set, by the law of the lot, to storm the seven gates of
our hold!
Be near and befriend us, O Pallas, the Zeus-born maiden
of might!
O lord of the steed and the sea, be thy trident uplifted to
smite
In eager desire of the fray, Poseidon! and Ares come down,
In fatherly presence revealed, to rescue Harmonia's town![2]
Thine too, Aphrodite, we are! thou art mother and queen
of our race,
To thee we cry out in our need, from thee let thy children
have grace!
Ye too, to scare back the foe, be your cry as a wolf's howl
wild,
Thou, O the wolf-lord, and thou, of she-wolf Leto the
child!
Woe and alack for the sound, for the rattle of cars to the
wall,
And the creak of the griding axles! O Hera, to thee is our
call!
Artemis, maiden beloved! the air is distraught with the
spears,
And whither doth destiny drive us, and where is the goal
of our fears?
The blast of the terrible stones on the ridge of our wall is
not stayed,

---

[2]Harmonia, the daughter of Ares (god of war) and Aphrodite (goddess of love),
was married to Cadmus and so might be considered mother of Thebes.

At the gates is the brazen clash of the bucklers—Apollo to
    aid!
Thou too, O daughter of Zeus, who guidest the wavering
    fray
To the holy decision of fate, Athena! be with us to-day!
Come down to the sevenfold gates and harry the foemen
    away!
O gods and O sisters of gods, our bulwark and guard! we
    beseech
That ye give not our war-worn hold to a rabble of alien
    speech!
List to the call of the maidens, the hands held up for the
    right,
Be near us, protect us, and show that the city is dear in
    your sight!
Have heed for her sacrifice holy, and thought of her offer-
    ings take,
Forget not her love and her worship, be near her and
    smite for her sake!

[*Re-enter* ETEOCLES.]

ETEOCLES

Hark to my question, things detestable!
Is this aright and for the city's weal,
And helpful to our army thus beset,
That ye before the statues of our gods
Should fling yourselves, and scream and shriek your fears?
Immodest, uncontrolled! Be this my lot—
Never in troublous nor in peaceful days
To dwell with aught that wears a female form!
Where womankind has power, no man can house,
Where womankind feeds panic, ruin rules
Alike in house and city! Look you now—
Your flying feet, and rumour of your fears,
Have spread a soulless panic on our walls,
And they without do go from strength to strength,
And we within make breach upon ourselves!
Such fate it brings, to house with womankind.

Therefore if any shall resist my rule—
Or man, or woman, or some sexless thing—
The vote of sentence shall decide their doom,
And stones of execution, past escape,
Shall finish all. Let not a woman's voice
Be loud in council! for the things without,
A man must care; let women keep within—
Even then is mischief all too probable!
Hear ye? or speak I to unheeding ears?

CHORUS

Ah, but I shudder, child of Oedipus!
    I heard the clash and clang!
The axles rolled and rumbled; woe to us
    Fire-welded bridles rang!

ETEOCLES

Say—when a ship is strained and deep in brine,
Did e'er a seaman mend his chance, who left
The helm, t' invoke the image at the prow?

CHORUS

Ah, but I fled to the shrines, I called to our helpers on
    high,
    When the stone-shower roared at the portals!
I sped to the temples aloft, and loud was my call and my
    cry,
    "Look down and deliver, Immortals!"

ETEOCLES

Ay, pray amain that stone may vanquish steel!
Were not that grace of gods? ay, ay—methinks,
When cities fall, the gods go forth from them!

CHORUS

Ah, let me die, or ever I behold
    The gods go forth, in conflagration dire!

The foemen's rush and raid, and all our hold
              Wrapt in the burning fire!

ETEOCLES

    Cry not on Heaven, in impotent debate!
    What saith the saw?—"Good saving Strength, in verity,
    Out of Obedience breeds the babe Prosperity."

CHORUS

    'Tis true: yet stronger is the power divine,
        And oft, when man's estate is overbowed
    With bitter pangs, disperses from his eyne
        The heavy, hanging cloud!

ETEOCLES

    Let men with sacrifice and augury
    Approach the gods, when comes the tug of war:
    Maids must be silent and abide within.

CHORUS

    By grace of the gods we hold it, a city untamed of the
        spear,
    And the battlement wards from the wall the foe and his as-
        pect of fear!
            What need of displeasure herein?

ETEOCLES

    Ay, pay thy vows to Heaven; I grudge them not,
    But—so thou strike no fear into our men—
    Have calm at heart, nor be too much afraid.

CHORUS

    Alack, it is fresh in mine ears, the clamour and crash of
        the fray,
    And up to our holiest height I sped on my timorous way,
            Bewildered, beset by the din!

ETEOCLES

Now, if ye hear the bruit of death or wounds,
Give not yourselves o'ermuch to shriek and scream,
For Ares ravins upon human flesh.

CHORUS

Ah, but the snorting of the steeds I hear!

ETEOCLES

Then, if thou hearest, hear them not too well!

CHORUS

Hark, the earth rumbles, as they close us round!

ETEOCLES

Enough if I am here, with plans prepared.

CHORUS

Alack, the battering at the gates is loud!

ETEOCLES

Peace! stay your tongue, or else the town may hear!

CHORUS

O warders of the walls, betray them not!

ETEOCLES

Beshrew your cries! in silence face your fate.

CHORUS

Gods of our city, see me not enslaved!

ETEOCLES

On me, on all, thy cries bring slavery.

CHORUS

Zeus, strong to smite, turn upon foes thy blow!

ETEOCLES

Zeus, what a curse are women, wrought by thee!

CHORUS

Weak wretches, even as men, when cities fall.

ETEOCLES

What! clasping gods, yet voicing thy despair?

CHORUS

In the sick heart, fear maketh prey of speech.

ETEOCLES

Light is the thing I ask thee—do my will!

CHORUS

Ask swiftly: swiftly shall I know my power.

ETEOCLES

Silence, weak wretch! nor put thy friends in fear.

CHORUS

I speak no more: the general fate be mine!

ETEOCLES

I take that word as wiser than the rest.
Nay, more: these images possess thy will—
Pray, in their strength, that Heaven be on our side!
Then hear my prayers withal, and then ring out
The female triumph-note, thy privilege—
Yea, utter forth the usage Hellas knows,

The cry beside the altars, sounding clear
Encouragement to friends, alarm to foes.
But I unto all gods that guard our walls,
Lords of the plain or warders of the mart
And to Ismenus' stream and Dirce's rills,[3]
I swear, if Fortune smiles and saves our town,
That we will make our altars reek with blood
Of sheep and kine, shed forth unto the gods,
And with victorious tokens front our fanes—
Corslets and casques that once our foemen wore,
Spear-shattered now—to deck these holy homes!
Be such thy vows to Heaven—away with sighs,
Away with outcry vain and barbarous,
That shall avail not, in a general doom!
But I will back, and, with six chosen men
Myself the seventh, to confront the foe
In this great aspect of a poisèd war,
Return and plant them at the sevenfold gates,
Or e'er the prompt and clamorous battle-scouts
Haste to inflame our counsel with the need.

[*Exit* ETEOCLES.]

CHORUS

  I mark his words, yet, dark and deep,
  My heart's alarm forbiddeth sleep!
  Close-clinging cares around my soul
  Enkindle fears beyond control,
  Presageful of what doom may fall
  From the great leaguer of the wall!
  So a poor dove is faint with fear
  For her weak nestlings, while anew
  Glides on the snaky ravisher!
  In troop and squadron, hand on hand,
  They climb and throng, and hemmed we stand,

[3]Ismenus and Dirce, both rivers of Thebes, were sacred to the city's
inhabitants.

While on the warders of our town
The flinty shower comes hurtling down!

Gods born of Zeus! put forth your might
For Cadmus' city, realm, and right!
What nobler land shall e'er be yours,
If once ye give to hostile powers
The deep rich soil, and Dirce's wave,
The nursing stream, Poseidon gave
And Tethys' children?[4] Up and save!
Cast on the ranks that hem us round
A deadly panic, make them fling
Their arms in terror on the ground,
And die in carnage! thence shall spring
High honour for our clan and king!
Come at our wailing cry, and stand
As thronèd sentries of our land!

For pity and sorrow it were that this immemorial town
Should sink to be slave of the spear, to dust and to ashes
   gone down,
By the gods of Achaean worship and arms of Achaean
   might
Sacked and defiled and dishonoured, its women the prize
   of the fight—
That, haled by the hair as a steed, their mantles dishev-
   elled and torn,
The maiden and matron alike should pass to the wedlock
   of scorn!
I hear it arise from the city, the manifold wail of despair—
"Woe, woe for the doom that shall be"—as in grasp of the
   foeman they fare!
For a woe and a weeping it is, if the maiden inviolate
   flower
Is plucked by the foe in his might, not culled in the bridal
   bower!

---

[4]Tethys was a titaness credited with great fertility.

Alas for the hate and the horror—how say it?—less hateful
    by far
Is the doom to be slain by the sword, hewn down in the
    carnage of war!
For wide, ah! wide is the woe when the foeman has
    mounted the wall;
There is havoc and terror and flame, and the dark smoke
    broods over all,
And wild is the war-god's breath, as in frenzy of conquest
    he springs,
And pollutes with the blast of his lips the glory of holiest
    things!

    Up to the citadel rise clash and din,
       The war-net closes in,
    The spear is in the heart: with blood imbrued
       Young mothers wail aloud,
    For children at their breast who scream and die!
       And boys and maidens fly,
    Yet scape not the pursuer, in his greed
       To thrust and grasp and feed!
    Robber with robber joins, each calls his mate
       Unto the feast of hate—
    "The banquet, lo! is spread—seize, rend, and tear!
       No need to choose or share!"
    And all the wealth of earth to waste is poured—
       A sight by all abhorred!
    The grieving housewives eye it; heaped and blent,
       Earth's boons are spoiled and spent,
    And waste to nothingness; and O alas,
       Young maids, forlorn ye pass—
    Fresh horror at your hearts—beneath the power
       Of those who crop the flower!
    Ye own the ruffian ravisher for lord,
       And night brings rites abhorred!
    Woe, woe for you! upon your grief and pain
       There comes a fouler stain.

          [Enter, on one side, THE SPY; *on the*
        other, ETEOCLES *and the* SIX CHAMPIONS.]

SEMI-CHORUS

> Look, friends! methinks the scout, who parted hence
> To spy upon the foemen, comes with news,
> His feet as swift as wafting chariot-wheels.

SEMI-CHORUS

> Ay, and our king, the son of Oedipus,
> Comes prompt to time, to learn the spy's report—
> His heart is fainer than his foot is fast!

THE SPY

> Well have I scanned the foe, and well can say
> Unto which chief, by lot, each gate is given.
> Tydeus[5] already with his onset-cry
> Storms at the gate called Proetides; but him
> The seer Amphiaraus[6] holds at halt,
> Nor wills that he should cross Ismenus' ford,
> Until the sacrifices promise fair.
> But Tydeus, mad with lust of blood and broil,
> Like to a cockatrice at noontide hour,
> Hisses out wrath and smites with scourge of tongue
> The prophet-son of Oecleus—"Wise thou art,
> Faint against war, and holding back from death!"
> With such revilings loud upon his lips
> He waves the triple plumes that o'er his helm
> Float overshadowing, as a courser's mane;

[5]For a discussion of the seven Argive warriors, their seven Theban opponents, and the seven gates at which they met, see the introductory note to this edition. Tydeus, by legend, had defeated many Thebans in competitive sports and had powerfully defended himself when a group of them later attacked him to even the score.

[6]Amphiaraus, a priest and a prophet, foresaw the end of the siege on Thebes, and was therefore perhaps the only Argive opposed to attacking Thebes. However, he'd made a pledge upon his marriage to the daughter of Adrastus that any disagreement between himself and her father would be settled by her judgment. In this case, his wife was bribed by Polynices to push Amphiaraus to join Adrustus's forces against Thebes. He chose to keep his marriage pledge, but went to his grave, as the legend has it, cursing his wife. His name means "very sacred."

And at his shield's rim, terror in their tone,
Clang and reverberate the brazen bells.
And this proud sign, wrought on his shield, he bears—
The vault of heaven, inlaid with blazing stars;
And, for the boss, the bright moon glows at full,
The eye of night, the first and lordliest star.
Thus with high-vaunted armour, madly bold,
He clamours by the stream-bank, wild for war,
As a steed panting grimly on his bit,
Held in and chafing for the trumpet's bray!
Whom wilt thou set against him? when the gates
Of Proetus yield, who can his rush repel?

ETEOCLES

To me, no blazon on a foeman's shield
Shall e'er present a fear! such pointed threats
Are powerless to wound; his plumes and bells,
Without a spear, are snakes without a sting.
Nay, more—that pageant of which thou tellest—
The nightly sky displayed, ablaze with stars,
Upon his shield, palters with double sense—
One headstrong fool will find its truth anon!
For, if night fall upon his eyes in death,
Yon vaunting blazon will its own truth prove,
And he is prophet of his folly's fall.
Mine shall it be, to pit against his power
The loyal son of Astacus, as guard
To hold the gateways—a right valiant soul,
Who has in heed the throne of Modesty
And loathes the speech of Pride, and evermore
Shrinks from the base, but knows no other fear.
He springs by stock from those whom Ares spared,
The men called Sown,[7] a right son of the soil,

---

[7]This is a reference to the legend of the origins of Thebes: Cadmus defeated a dragon that was terrorizing the area. He then took the dragon's teeth and threw them across the soil, where they took root. From them grew up a crowd of armed men—the "sown" men—who began immediately to fight and kill each other. The ones who survived ("whom Ares spared") were considered the first of the city's nobility.

And Melanippus styled. Now, what his arm
To-day shall do, rests with the dice of war,
And Ares shall ordain it; but his cause
Hath the true badge of Right, to urge him on
To guard, as son, his motherland from wrong.

CHORUS

> Then may the gods give fortune fair
> Unto our chief, sent forth to dare
>   War's terrible arbitrament!
> But ah! when champions wend away,
> I shudder, lest, from out the fray,
>   Only their blood-stained wrecks be sent!

THE SPY

Nay, let him pass, and the gods' help be his!
Next, Capaneus[8] comes on, by lot to lead
The onset at the gates Electran styled:
A giant he, more huge than Tydeus' self,
And more than human in his arrogance—
May fate forefend his threat against our walls!
"God willing, or unwilling"—such his vaunt—
"I will lay waste this city; Pallas' self,
Zeus' warrior maid, although she swoop to earth
And plant her in my path, shall stay me not."
And, for the flashes of the levin-bolt,
He holds them harmless as the noontide rays.
Mark, too, the symbol on his shield—a man
Scornfully weaponless but torch in hand,
And the flame glows within his grasp, prepared
For ravin: lo, the legend, wrought in words,
"Fire for the city bring I," flares in gold!
Against such wight, send forth—yet whom? what man
Will front that vaunting figure and not fear?

---

[8]The name Capaneus suggests smoke—a fitting connotation, since it was believed that Zeus killed him personally, with a thunderbolt.

ETEOCLES

Aha, this profits also, gain on gain!
In sooth, for mortals, the tongue's utterance
Bewrays unerringly a foolish pride!
Hither stalks Capaneus, with vaunt and threat
Defying god-like powers, equipt to act,
And, mortal though he be, he strains his tongue
In folly's ecstasy, and casts aloft
High swelling words against the ears of Zeus.
Right well I trust—if justice grants the word—
That, by the might of Zeus, a bolt of flame
In more than semblance shall descend on him.
Against his vaunts, though reckless, I have set,
To make assurance sure, a warrior stern—
Strong Polyphontes,[9] fervid for the fray;—
A sturdy bulwark, he, by grace of Heaven
And favour of his champion Artemis!
Say on, who holdeth the next gate in ward?

CHORUS

Perish the wretch whose vaunt affronts our home!
    On him the red bolt come,
Ere to the maiden bowers his way he cleave,
    To ravage and bereave!

THE SPY

I will say on. Eteoclus[10] is third—
To him it fell, what time the third lot sprang
O'er the inverted helmet's brazen rim,
To dash his stormers on Neïstae gate.
He wheels his mares, who at their frontlets chafe
And yearn to charge upon the gates amain.
They snort the breath of pride, and, filled therewith,
Their nozzles whistle with barbaric sound.

[9]Polyphontes means "killer of many."
[10]It has been suggested that this Argive warrior, whose name is so remarkably close to Eteocles's represents Eteocles as his own enemy.

High too and haughty is his shield's device—
An armèd man who climbs, from rung to rung,
A scaling ladder, up a hostile wall,
Afire to sack and slay; and he too cries,
(By letters, full of sound, upon the shield)
"Not Ares' self shall cast me from the wall."
Look to it, send, against this man, a man
Strong to debar the slave's joke from our town.

ETEOCLES (*pointing to* MEGAREUS)

Send will I—even this man, with luck to aid—
By his worth sent already, not by pride
And vain pretence, is he. 'Tis Megareus,
The child of Creon,[11] of the Earth-sprung born!
He will not shrink from guarding of the gates,
Nor fear the maddened charger's frenzied neigh,
But, if he dies, will nobly quit the score
For nurture to the land that gave him birth,
Or from the shield-side hew two warriors down—
Eteoclus and the figure that he lifts—
Ay, and the city pictured, all in one,
And deck with spoils the temple of his sire!
Announce the next pair, stint not of thy tongue!

CHORUS

O thou, the warder of my home,
    Grant, unto us, Fate's favouring tide,
Send on the foemen doom!
    They fling forth taunts of frenzied pride,
On them may Zeus with glare of vengeance come!

THE SPY

Lo, next him stands a fourth and shouts amain,
By Pallas Onca's[12] portal, and displays

[11]Creon was uncle to Eteocles and Polynices, therefore Megareus was their first cousin.
[12]*Pallas Onca* a regional name for Athena.

A different challenge; 'tis Hippomedon!
Huge the device that starts up from his targe
In high relief; and, I deny it not,
I shuddered, seeing how, upon the rim,
It made a mighty circle round the shield—
No sorry craftsman he, who wrought that work
And clamped it all around the buckler's edge!
The form was Typhon:[13] from his glowing throat
Rolled lurid smoke, spark-litten, kin of fire!
The flattened edge-work, circling round the whole,
Made strong support for coiling snakes that grew
Erect above the concave of the shield:
Loud rang the warrior's voice; inspired for war,
He raves to slay, as doth a Bacchanal,
His very glance a terror! of such wight
Beware the onset! closing on the gates,
He peals his vaunting and appalling cry!

ETEOCLES

Yet first our Pallas Onca—wardress she,
Planting her foot hard by her gate—shall stand,
The Maid against the ruffian, and repel
His force, as from her brood the mother-bird
Beats back the wintered serpent's venom'd fang.
And next, by her, is Oenops' gallant son,
Hyperbius, chosen to confront this foe,
Ready to seek his fate at Fortune's shrine!
In form, in valour, and in skill of arms,
None shall gainsay him. See how wisely well
Hermes hath set the brave against the strong!
Confronted shall they stand, the shield of each
Bearing the image of opposing gods:
One holds aloft his Typhon breathing fire,
But, on the other's shield, in symbol sits
Zeus, calm and strong, and fans his bolt to flame—
Zeus, seen of all, yet seen of none to fail!
Howbeit, weak is trust reposed in Heaven—

---

[13]A typhon was a monster with one hundred dragon-shaped heads.

Yet are we upon Zeus' victorious side,
The foe, with those he worsted—if in sooth
Zeus against Typhon held the upper hand,
And if Hyperbius, (as well may hap
When two such foes such diverse emblems bear)
Have Zeus upon his shield, a saving sign.

CHORUS

High faith is mine that he whose shield
Bears, against Zeus, the thing of hate.
The giant Typhon, thus revealed,
A monster loathed of gods eterne
And mortal men—this doom shall earn
A shattered skull, before the gate!

THE SPY

Heaven send it so! A fifth assailant now
Is set against our fifth, the northern, gate,
Fronting the death-mound where Amphion[14] lies
The child of Zeus. This foeman vows his faith,
Upon a mystic spear-head which he deems
More holy than a godhead and more sure
To find its mark than any glance of eye,
That, will they, nill they, he will storm and sack
The hold of the Cadmeans. Such his oath—
His, the bold warrior, yet of childish years,
A bud of beauty's foremost flower, the son
Of Zeus and of the mountain maid. I mark
How the soft down is waxing on his cheek,
Thick and close-growing in its tender prime—
In name, not mood, is he a maiden's child—
Parthenopaeus;[15] large and bright his eyes

---

[14]Amphion and his brother Zethus were credited with having walled the city
of Thebes.

[15]Parthenopaeus means "maiden-faced." His name and appearance recall his
mother the mountain (Arcadian) maiden Atalanta, but his fierce fighting
spirit seems to come from his father, Zeus.

But fierce the wrath wherewith he fronts the gate:
Yet not unheralded he takes his stand
Before the portal; on his brazen shield,
The rounded screen and shelter of his form,
I saw him show the ravening Sphinx,[16] the fiend
That shamed our city—how it glared and moved,
Clamped on the buckler, wrought in high relief!
And in its claws did a Cadmean bear—
Nor heretofore, for any single prey,
Sped she aloft, through such a storm of darts
As now awaits her. So our foe is here—
Like, as I deem, to play no stinted trade
In blood and broil, but traffick as is meet
In fierce exchange for his long wayfaring!

ETEOCLES

Ah, may they meet the doom they think to bring—
They and their impious vaunts—from those on high!
So should they sink, hurled down to deepest death!
This foe, at least, by thee Arcadian styled,[17]
Is faced by one who bears no braggart sign,
But his hand sees to smite, where blows avail—
Actor, own brother to Hyperbius!
He will not let a boast without a blow
Stream through our gates and nourish our despair,
Nor give him way who on his hostile shield
Bears the brute image of the loathly Sphinx!
Blocked at the gate, she will rebuke the man
Who strives to thrust her forward, when she feels
Thick crash of blows, up to the city wall.
With Heaven's goodwill, my forecast shall be true.

---

[16]The Sphinx had held the people of Thebes in deprivation until Oedipus defeated her by answering her riddle. It was this act that won him the throne of Thebes and its queen—his own mother—as his wife and mother of his own children.

[17]Arcadia was a remote, mountainous region.

CHORUS

> Home to my heart the vaunting goes,
>   And, quick with terror, on my head
> Rises my hair, at sound of those
>   Who wildly, impiously rave!
> If gods there be, to them I plead—
>   "Give them to darkness and the grave."

THE SPY

> Fronting the sixth gate stands another foe,
> Wisest of warriors, bravest among seers—
> Such must I name Amphiaraus: he,
> Set steadfast at the Homoloïd gate,
> Berates strong Tydeus with reviling words—
> "The man of blood, the bane of state and home,
> To Argos, arch-allurer to all ill,
> Evoker of the fury-fiend of hell,
> Death's minister, and counsellor of wrong
> Unto Adrastus in this fatal field."
> Ay, and with eyes upturned and mien of scorn
> He chides thy brother Polynices too
> At his desert, and once and yet again
> Dwells hard and meaningly upon his name[18]
> Where it saith "glory" yet importeth "feud."
> "Yea, such thou art in act, and such thy grace
> In sight of Heaven, and such in aftertime
> Thy fame, for lips and ears of mortal men!
> "He strove to sack the city of his sires
> And temples of her gods, and brought on her
> An alien armament of foreign foes.
> The fountain of maternal blood outpoured
> What power can staunch? even so, thy fatherland
> Once by thine ardent malice stormed and ta'en,
> Shall ne'er join force with thee." For me, I know
> It doth remain to let my blood enrich

---

[18]Polynices means "much strife."

The border of this land that loves me not—
Blood of a prophet, in a foreign grave!
Now, for the battle! I foreknow my doom,
Yet it shall be with honour." So he spake,
The prophet, holding up his targe of bronze
Wrought without blazon, to the ears of men
Who stood around and heeded not his word.
For on no bruit and rumour of great deeds,
But on their doing, is his spirit set,
And in his heart he reaps a furrow rich,
Wherefrom the foison of good counsel springs.
Against him, send brave heart and hand of might,
For the god-lover is man's fiercest foe.

ETEOCLES

Out on the chance that couples mortal men,
Linking the just and impious in one!
In every issue, the one curse is this—
Companionship with men of evil heart!
A baneful harvest, let none gather it!
The field of sin is rank, and brings forth death
At whiles a righteous man who goes aboard
With reckless mates, a horde of villainy,
Dies by one death with that detested crew;
At whiles the just man, joined with citizens
Ruthless to strangers, recking nought of Heaven,
Trapped, against nature, in one net with them,
Dies by God's thrust and all-including blow.
So will this prophet die, even Oecleus' child,
Sage, just, and brave, and loyal towards Heaven,
Potent in prophecy, but mated here
With men of sin, too boastful to be wise!
Long is their road, and they return no more,
And, at their taking-off, by hand of Zeus,
The prophet too shall take the downward way.
He will not—so I deem—assail the gate—
Not as through cowardice or feeble will,
But as one knowing to what end shall be
Their struggle in the battle, if indeed

Fruit of fulfilment lie in Loxias'[19] word.
He speaketh not, unless to speak avails!
Yet, for more surety, we will post a man,
Strong Lasthenes, as warder of the gate,
Stern to the foeman; he hath age's skill,
Mated with youthful vigour, and an eye
Forward, alert; swift too his hand, to catch
The fenceless interval 'twixt shield and spear!
Yet man's good fortune lies in hand of Heaven.

CHORUS

Unto our loyal cry, ye gods, give ear!
Save, save the city! turn away the spear,
Send on the foemen fear!
Outside the rampart fall they, rent and riven
Beneath the bolt of heaven!

THE SPY

Last, let me name yon seventh antagonist,
Thy brother's self, at the seventh portal set—
Hear with what wrath he imprecates our doom,
Vowing to mount the wall, though banished hence,
And peal aloud the wild exulting cry—
"The town is ta'en"—then clash his sword with thine,
Giving and taking death in close embrace,
Or, if thou 'scapest, flinging upon thee,
As robber of his honour and his home,
The doom of exile such as he has borne.
So clamours he and so invokes the gods
Who guard his race and home, to hear and heed
The curse that sounds in Polynices' name!
He bears a round shield, fresh from forge and fire,
And wrought upon it is a twofold sign—
For lo, a woman leads decorously
The figure of a warrior wrought in gold;
And thus the legend runs—"I Justice am,

---

[19]*Loxias* Apollo.

And I will bring the hero home again,
To hold once more his place within this town,
Once more to pace his sire's ancestral hall."
Such are the symbols, by our foemen shown—
Now make thine own decision, whom to send
Against this last opponent! I have said—
Nor canst thou in my tidings find a flaw—
Thine is it, now, to steer the course aright.

ETEOCLES

Ah me, the madman, and the curse of Heaven!
And woe for us, the lamentable line
Of Oedipus, and woe that in this house
Our father's curse must find accomplishment!
But now, a truce to tears and loud lament,
Lest they should breed a still more rueful wail!
As for this Polynices, named too well,[20]
Soon shall we know how his device shall end—
Whether the gold-wrought symbols on his shield,
In their mad vaunting and bewildered pride,
Shall guide him as a victor to his home!
For had but Justice, maiden-child of Zeus,
Stood by his act and thought, it might have been!
Yet never, from the day he reached the light
Out of the darkness of his mother's womb,
Never in childhood, nor in youthful prime,
Nor when his chin was gathering its beard,
Hath Justice hailed or claimed him as her own.
Therefore I deem not that she standeth now
To aid him in this outrage on his home!
Misnamed, in truth, were Justice, utterly,
If to impiety she lent her hand.
Sure in this faith, I will myself go forth
And match me with him; who hath fairer claim?
Ruler, against one fain to snatch the rule,
Brother with brother matched, and foe with foe,
Will I confront the issue. To the wall!

[20]See note 18, p. 22.

CHORUS

> O thou true heart, O child of Oedipus,
> Be not, in wrath, too like the man whose name
> Murmurs an evil omen! 'Tis enough
> That Cadmus' clan should strive with Argos' host,
> For blood there is that can atone that stain!
> But—brother upon brother dealing death—
> Not time itself can expiate the sin!

ETEOCLES

> If man find hurt, yet clasp his honour still,
> 'Tis well; the dead have honour, nought beside.
> Hurt, with dishonour, wins no word of praise!

CHORUS

> Ah, what is thy desire?
> Let not the lust and ravin of the sword
> Bear thee adown the tide accursed, abhorred!
> Fling off thy passion's rage, thy spirit's prompting dire!

ETEOCLES

> Nay—since the god is urgent for our doom,
> Let Laïus' house, by Phoebus loathed and scorned,
> Follow the gale of destiny, and win
> Its great inheritance, the gulf of hell!

CHORUS

> Ruthless thy craving is—
> Craving for kindred and forbidden blood
> To be outpoured—a sacrifice imbrued
> With sin, a bitter fruit of murderous enmities!

ETEOCLES

> Yea, my own father's fateful Curse proclaims—
> A ghastly presence, and her eyes are dry—
> "Strike! honour is the prize, not life prolonged!"

CHORUS

> Ah, be not urged of her! for none shall dare
> To call thee "coward," in thy throned estate!
> Will not the Fury in her sable pall
> Pass outward from these halls, what time the gods
> Welcome a votive offering from our hands?

ETEOCLES

> The gods! long since they hold us in contempt,
> Scornful of gifts thus offered by the lost!
> Why should we fawn and flinch away from doom?

CHORUS

> Now, when it stands beside thee! for its power
> May, with a changing gust of milder mood,
> Temper the blast that bloweth wild and rude
>   And frenzied, in this hour!

ETEOCLES

> Ay, kindled by the curse of Oedipus—
> All too prophetic, out of dreamland came
> The vision, meting out our sire's estate!

CHORUS

> Heed women's voices, though thou love them not!

ETEOCLES

> Say aught that may avail, but stint thy words.

CHORUS

> Go not thou forth to guard the seventh gate!

ETEOCLES

> Words shall not blunt the edge of my resolve.

CHORUS

Yet the god loves to let the weak prevail.

ETEOCLES

That to a swordsman, is no welcome word!

CHORUS

Shall thine own brother's blood be victory's palm?

ETEOCLES

Ill which the gods have sent thou canst not shun!

[*Exit* ETEOCLES.]

CHORUS

I shudder in dread of the power, abhorred by the gods of
high heaven,
The ruinous curse of the home till roof-tree and rafter be
riven!
Too true are the visions of ill, too true the fulfilment they
bring
To the curse that was spoken of old by the frenzy and
wrath of the king!
Her will is the doom of the children, and Discord is kin-
dled amain,
And strange is the Lord of Division, who cleaveth the
birthright in twain,—
The edged thing, born of the north, the steel that is ruthless and keen,
Dividing in bitter division the lot of the children of teen!
Not the wide lowland around, the realm of their sire, shall
they have,
Yet enough for the dead to inherit, the pitiful space of a
grave!

Ah, but when kin meets kin, when sire and child,
    Unknowing, are defiled
By shedding common blood, and when the pit
    Of death devoureth it,
Drinking the clotted stain, the gory dye—
    Who, who can purify?
Who cleanse pollution, where the ancient bane
    Rises and reeks again?
Whilome in olden days the sin was wrought,
    And swift requital brought—
Yea on the children of the child came still
    New heritage of ill!
For thrice Apollo spoke this word divine,
    From Delphi's central shrine,
To Laïus—"Die thou childless! thus alone
    Can the land's weal be won!"
But vainly with his wife's desire he strove,
    And gave himself to love,
Begetting Oedipus, by whom he died,
    The fateful parricide!
The sacred seed-plot, his own mother's womb,
    He sowed, his house's doom,
A root of blood! by frenzy lured, they came
    Unto their wedded shame.
And now the waxing surge, the wave of fate,
    Rolls on them, triply great—
One billow sinks, the next towers, high and dark,
    Above our city's bark—
Only the narrow barrier of the wall
    Totters, as soon to fall;
And, if our chieftains in the storm go down,
    What chance can save the town?
Curses, inherited from long ago,
    Bring heavy freight of woe:
Rich stores of merchandise o'erload the deck,
    Near, nearer comes the wreck—
And all is lost, cast out upon the wave,
    Floating, with none to save!

Whom did the gods, whom did the chief of men,
    Whom did each citizen
In crowded concourse, in such honour hold,
    As Oedipus of old,
When the grim fiend, that fed on human prey,
    He took from us away?

But when, in the fulness of days, he knew of his bridal un-
    blest,
A twofold horror he wrought, in the frenzied despair of his
    breast—
Debarred from the grace of the banquet, the service of
    goblets of gold,
He flung on his children a curse for the splendour they
    dared to withhold,
A curse prophetic and bitter—"The glory of wealth and of
    pride,
With iron, not gold, in your hands, ye shall come, at the
    last, to divide!"
Behold, how a shudder runs through me, lest now, in the
    fulness of time,
The house-fiend awake and return, to mete out the mea-
    sure of crime!

                             [*Enter* THE SPY.]

THE SPY

Take heart, ye daughters whom your mothers' milk
Made milky-hearted! lo, our city stands,
Saved from the yoke of servitude: the vaunts
Of overweening men are silent now,
And the State sails beneath a sky serene,
Nor in the manifold and battering waves
Hath shipped a single surge, and solid stands
The rampart, and the gates are made secure,
Each with a single champion's trusty guard.
So in the main and at six gates we hold
A victory assured; but, at the seventh,
The god that on the seventh day was born,
Royal Apollo, hath ta'en up his rest

To wreak upon the sons of Oedipus
Their grandsire's wilfulness of long ago.

CHORUS

What further woefulness besets our home?

THE SPY

The home stands safe—but ah, the princes twain—

CHORUS

Who? what of them? I am distraught with fear.

THE SPY

Hear now, and mark! the sons of Oedipus—

CHORUS

Ah, my prophetic soul! I feel their doom.

THE SPY

Have done with questions!—with their lives crushed out—

CHORUS

Lie they out yonder? the full horror speak!
Did hands meet hands more close than brotherly?
Came fate on each, and in the selfsame hour?

THE SPY

Yea, blotting out the lineage ill-starred!
Now mix your exultation and your tears,
Over a city saved, the while its lords,
Twin leaders of the fight, have parcelled out
With forged arbitrament of Scythian steel
The full division of their fatherland,
And, as their father's imprecation bade,

Shall have their due of land, a twofold grave.
So is the city saved; the earth has drunk
Blood of twin princes, by each other slain.

CHORUS

O mighty Zeus and guardian powers,
The strength and stay of Cadmus' towers!
Shall I send forth a joyous cry,
　"Hail to the lord of weal renewed?"
Or weep the misbegotten twain,
Born to a fatal destiny?
Each numbered now among the slain,
　Each dying in ill fortitude,
Each "truly named," each "child of feud?"

O dark and all-prevailing ill,
　That broods o'er Oedipus and all his line,
Numbing my heart with mortal chill!
　Ah me, this song of mine,
Which, Thyad-like[21] I woke, now falleth still,
　Or only tells of doom,
　And echoes round a tomb!
Dead are they, dead! in their own blood they lie—
Ill-omened the concent that hails our victory!
The curse a father on his children spake
　Hath faltered not, nor failed!
Nought, Laïus! thy stubborn choice availed—
First to beget, then, in the after day
　　And for the city's sake,
　　The child to slay!
　　For nought can blunt nor mar
　　The speech oracular!
　Children of teen! by disbelief ye erred—
Yet in wild weeping came fulfilment of the word!

> [ANTIGONE *and* ISMENE *approach, with
> a train of mourners, bearing the bodies
> of* ETEOCLES *and* POLYNICES.]

---

[21]*Thyad-like* rage-like.

Look up, look forth! the doom is plain,
Nor spake the messenger in vain!
A twofold sorrow, twofold strife—
Each brave against a brother's life!
In double doom hath sorrow come—
How shall I speak it?—on the home!
Alas, my sisters! be your sighs the gale,
The smiting of your brows the plash of oars,
Wafting the boat, to Acheron's[22] dim shores
That passeth ever, with its darkened sail,
On its uncharted voyage and sunless way,
Far from thy beams, Apollo, god of day—
    The melancholy bark
Bound for the common bourn, the harbour of the
    dark!

Look up, look yonder! from the home
Antigone, Ismene come,
On the last, saddest errand bound,
To chant a dirge of doleful sound,
With agony of equal pain
Above their brethren slain!
Their sister-bosoms surely swell,
Heart with rent heart according well
In grief for those who fought and fell!
Yet—ere they utter forth their woe—
We must awake the rueful strain
To vengeful powers, in realms below,
And mourn hell's triumph o'er the slain!

Alas! of all, the breast who bind,—
Yea, all the race of womankind—
    O maidens, ye are most bereaved!
For you, for you the tear-drops start—
    Deem that in truth, and undeceived,
Ye hear the sorrows of my heart!
    (*To the dead.*)

---

[22]*Acheron* a river which the Greeks believed formed the entrance to Hades.

Children of bitterness, and sternly brave—
    One, proud of heart against persuasion's voice,
    One, against exile proof! ye win your choice—
Each in your fatherland, a separate grave!

    Alack, on house and heritage
They brought a baneful doom, and death for wage!
One strove through tottering walls to force his way,
One claimed, in bitter arrogance, the sway,
    And both alike, even now and here,
Have closed their suit, with steel for arbiter!
    And lo, the Fury-fiend of Oedipus, their sire,
Hath brought his curse to consummation dire!
        Each in the left side smitten, see them laid—
            The children of one womb,
            Slain by a mutual doom!
Alas, their fate! the combat murderous,
    The horror of the house,
The curse of ancient bloodshed, now repaid!
Yea, deep and to the heart the deathblow fell,
    Edged by their feud ineffable—
By the grim curse, their sire did imprecate—
    Discord and deadly hate!
Hark, how the city and its towers make moan—
How the land mourns that held them for its own!
Fierce greed and fell division did they blend,
    Till death made end!
They strove to part the heritage in twain,
    Giving to each a gain—
Yet that which struck the balance in the strife,
    The arbitrating sword,
By those who loved the twain is held abhorred—
Loathed is the god of death, who sundered each
        from life!
    Here, by the stroke of steel, behold! they lie—
        And rightly may we cry
"Beside their fathers, let them here be laid—
Iron gave their doom, with iron their graves be made—
Alack, the slaying sword, alack, th' entombing spade!"

Alas, a piercing shriek, a rending groan,
A cry unfeigned of sorrow felt at heart!
With shuddering of grief, with tears that start,
With wailful escort, let them hither come—
For one or other make divided moan!
No light lament of pity mixed with gladness,
But with true tears, poured from the soul of sadness
Over the princes dead and their bereavèd home
Say we, above these brethren dead,
   "On citizen, on foreign foe,
Brave was their rush, and stern their blow—
   Now, lowly are they laid!"
Beyond all women upon earth
Woe, woe for her who gave them birth!
Unknowingly, her son she wed—
The children of that marriage-bed,
Each in the self-same womb, were bred—
Each by a brother's hand lies dead!

Yea, from one seed they sprang, and by one fate
    Their heritage is desolate,
  The heart's division sundered claim from claim,
    And, from their feud, death came!
    Now is their hate allayed,
    Now is their life-stream shed,
  Ensanguining the earth with crimson dye—
Lo, from one blood they sprang, and in one blood they lie!
A grievous arbiter was given the twain—
  The stranger from the northern main,
    The sharp, dividing sword,
    Fresh from the forge and fire
The War-god treacherous gave ill award
And brought their father's curse to a fulfilment dire!
  They have their portion—each his lot and doom,
    Given from the gods on high!
  Yea, the piled wealth of fatherland, for tomb,
    Shall underneath them lie!
  Alas, alas! with flowers of fame and pride
    Your home ye glorified;

But, in the end, the Furies gathered round
   With chants of boding sound,
Shrieking, "In wild defeat and disarray,
   Behold, ye pass away!"
The sign of Ruin standeth at the gate,
   There, where they strove with Fate—
And the ill power beheld the brothers' fall,
   And triumphed over all!

ANTIGONE, ISMENE, *and* CHORUS

(*Processional Chant*)

Thou wert smitten, in smiting,
   Thou didst slay, and wert slain—
By the spear of each other
   Ye lie on the plain,
And ruthless the deed that ye wrought was, and ruthless
   the death of the twain!

Take voice, O my sorrow!
   Flow tear upon tear—
Lay the slain by the slayer,
   Made one on the bier!
Our soul in distraction is lost, and we mourn o'er the prey
   of the spear!

Ah, woe for your ending,
   Unbrotherly wrought!
And woe for the issue,
   The fray that ye fought,
The doom of a mutual slaughter whereby to the grave ye
   are brought!

Ah, twofold the sorrow—
   The heard and the seen!
And double the tide
   Of our tears and our teen,
As we stand by our brothers in death and wail for the love
   that has been!

O grievous the fate
That attends upon wrong!
Stern ghost of our sire,
Thy vengeance is long!
Dark Fury of hell and of death, the hands of thy kingdom
are strong!

O dark were the sorrows
That exile hath known!
He slew, but returned not
Alive to his own!
He struck down a brother, but fell, in the moment of tri-
umph hewn down!

O lineage accurst,
O doom and despair!
Alas, for their quarrel,
The brothers that were!
And woe! for their pitiful end, who once were our love
and our care!

O grievous the fate
That attends upon wrong!
Stern ghost of our sire,
Thy vengeance is long!
Dark Fury of hell and of death, the hands of thy kingdom
are strong!

By proof have ye learnt it!
At once and as one,
O brothers belovèd,
To death ye were done!
Ye came to the strife of the sword, and behold! ye are both
overthrown!

O grievous the tale is,
And grievous their fall,
To the house, to the land,
And to me above all!
Ah God! for the curse that hath come, the sin and the ruin
withal!

O children distraught,
   Who in madness have died!
Shall ye rest with old kings
   In the place of their pride?
Alas for the wrath of your sire if he findeth you laid by his
   side!

[Enter a HERALD.*]*

HERALD

I bear command to tell to one and all
What hath approved itself and now is law,
Ruled by the counsellors of Cadmus' town.
For this Eteocles, it is resolved
To lay him on his earth-bed, in this soil,
Not without care and kindly sepulture.
For why? he hated those who hated us,
And, with all duties blamelessly performed
Unto the sacred ritual of his sires,
He met such end as gains our city's grace,—
With auspices that do ennoble death.
Such words I have in charge to speak of him:
But of his brother Polynices, this—
Be he cast out unburied, for the dogs
To rend and tear: for he presumed to waste
The land of the Cadmeans, had not Heaven—
Some god of those who aid our fatherland—
Opposed his onset, by his brother's spear,
To whom, tho' dead, shall consecration come!
Against him stood this wretch, and brought a horde
Of foreign foemen, to beset our town.
He therefore shall receive his recompense,
Buried ignobly in the maw of kites—
No women-wailers to escort his corpse
Nor pile his tomb nor shrill his dirge anew—
Unhouselled, unattended, cast away!
So, for these brothers, doth our State ordain.

ANTIGONE

>And I—to those who make such claims of rule
>In Cadmus' town—I, though no other help,
>   (*Pointing to the body of* POLYNICES)
>I, I will bury this my brother's corpse
>And risk your wrath and what may come of it!
>It shames me not to face the State, and set
>Will against power, rebellion resolute:
>Deep in my heart is set my sisterhood,
>My common birthright with my brothers, born
>All of one womb, her children who, for woe,
>Brought forth sad offspring to a sire ill-starred.
>Therefore, my soul! take thou thy willing share,
>In aid of him who now can will no more,
>Against this outrage: be a sister true,
>While yet thou livest, to a brother dead!
>Him never shall the wolves with ravening maw
>Rend and devour: I do forbid the thought!
>I for him, I—albeit a woman weak—
>In place of burial-pit, will give him rest
>By this protecting handful of light dust
>Which, in the lap of this poor linen robe,
>I bear to hallow and bestrew his corpse
>With the due covering. Let none gainsay!
>Courage and craft shall arm me, this to do.

HERALD

>I charge thee, not to flout the city's law!

ANTIGONE

>I charge thee, use no useless heralding!

HERALD

>Stern is a people newly 'scaped from death.

ANTIGONE

>Whet thou their sternness! burial he shall have.

HERALD

How? grace of burial, to the city's foe?

ANTIGONE

God hath not judged him separate in guilt.

HERALD

True—till he put this land in jeopardy.

ANTIGONE

His rights usurped, he answered wrong with wrong.

HERALD

Nay—but for one man's sin he smote the State.

ANTIGONE

Contention doth out-talk all other gods!
Prate thou no more—I will to bury him.

HERALD

Will, an thou wilt! but I forbid the deed.

[*Exit the* HERALD.]

CHORUS

Exulting Fates, who waste the line
   And whelm the house of Oedipus!
Fiends, who have slain, in wrath condign,
   The father and the children thus!
What now befits it that I do,
What meditate, what undergo?
Can I the funeral rite refrain,
Nor weep for Polynices slain?
But yet, with fear I shrink and thrill,
Presageful of the city's will!

Thou, O Eteocles, shalt have
Full rites, and mourners at thy grave,
But he, thy brother slain, shall he,
With none to weep or cry "Alas,"
To unbefriended burial pass?
Only one sister o'er his bier,
To raise the cry and pour the tear—
Who can obey such stern decree?

SEMI-CHORUS

Let those who hold our city's sway
    Wreak, or forbear to wreak, their will
On those who cry, "Ah, well-a-day!"
    Lamenting Polynices still!
We will go forth and, side by side
With her, due burial will provide!
Royal he was; to him be paid
Our grief, wherever he be laid!
The crowd may sway, and change, and still
Take its caprice for Justice' will!
But we this dead Eteocles,
As Justice wills and Right decrees,
    Will bear unto his grave!
For—under those enthroned on high
And Zeus' eternal royalty—
He unto us salvation gave!
    He saved us from a foreign yoke,—
    A wild assault of outland folk,
A savage, alien wave!

[*Exeunt.*]

DOVER · THRIFT · EDITIONS

POETRY

A SHROPSHIRE LAD, A. E. Housman. 64pp. 26468-8 $1.00

LYRIC POEMS, John Keats. 80pp. 26871-3 $1.00

GUNGA DIN AND OTHER FAVORITE POEMS, Rudyard Kipling. 80pp. 26471-8 $1.00

THE CONGO AND OTHER POEMS, Vachel Lindsay. 96pp. 27272-9 $1.50

EVANGELINE AND OTHER POEMS, Henry Wadsworth Longfellow. 64pp. 28255-4 $1.00

FAVORITE POEMS, Henry Wadsworth Longfellow. 96pp. 27273-7 $1.00

"TO HIS COY MISTRESS" AND OTHER POEMS, Andrew Marvell. 64pp. 29544-3 $1.00

SPOON RIVER ANTHOLOGY, Edgar Lee Masters. 144pp. 27275-3 $1.50

RENASCENCE AND OTHER POEMS, Edna St. Vincent Millay. 64pp. (Available in U.S. only.) 26873-X $1.00

SELECTED POEMS, John Milton. 128pp. 27554-X $1.50

CIVIL WAR POETRY: An Anthology, Paul Negri (ed.). 128pp. 29883-3 $1.50

ENGLISH VICTORIAN POETRY: AN ANTHOLOGY, Paul Negri (ed.). 256pp. 40425-0 $2.00

GREAT SONNETS, Paul Negri (ed.). 96pp. 28052-7 $1.00

THE RAVEN AND OTHER FAVORITE POEMS, Edgar Allan Poe. 64pp. 26685-0 $1.00

ESSAY ON MAN AND OTHER POEMS, Alexander Pope. 128pp. 28053-5 $1.50

EARLY POEMS, Ezra Pound. 80pp. (Available in U.S. only.) 28745-9 $1.00

GREAT POEMS BY AMERICAN WOMEN: An Anthology, Susan L. Rattiner (ed.). 224pp. (Available in U.S. only.) 40164-2 $2.00

LITTLE ORPHANT ANNIE AND OTHER POEMS, James Whitcomb Riley. 80pp. 28260-0 $1.00

"MINIVER CHEEVY" AND OTHER POEMS, Edwin Arlington Robinson. 64pp. 28756-4 $1.00

GOBLIN MARKET AND OTHER POEMS, Christina Rossetti. 64pp. 28055-1 $1.00

CHICAGO POEMS, Carl Sandburg. 80pp. 28057-8 $1.00

THE SHOOTING OF DAN MCGREW AND OTHER POEMS, Robert Service. 96pp. (Available in U.S. only.) 27556-6 $1.50

COMPLETE SONNETS, William Shakespeare. 80pp. 26686-9 $1.00

SELECTED POEMS, Percy Bysshe Shelley. 128pp. 27558-2 $1.50

AFRICAN-AMERICAN POETRY: An Anthology, 1773–1930, Joan R. Sherman (ed.). 96pp. 29604-0 $1.00

100 BEST-LOVED POEMS, Philip Smith (ed.). 96pp. 28553-7 $1.00

NATIVE AMERICAN SONGS AND POEMS: An Anthology, Brian Swann (ed.). 64pp. 29450-1 $1.00

SELECTED POEMS, Alfred Lord Tennyson. 112pp. 27282-6 $1.50

AENEID, Vergil (Publius Vergilius Maro). 256pp. 28749-1 $2.00

CHRISTMAS CAROLS: COMPLETE VERSES, Shane Weller (ed.). 64pp. 27397-0 $1.00

GREAT LOVE POEMS, Shane Weller (ed.). 128pp. 27284-2 $1.00

CIVIL WAR POETRY AND PROSE, Walt Whitman. 96pp. 28507-3 $1.00

SELECTED POEMS, Walt Whitman. 128pp. 26878-0 $1.00

THE BALLAD OF READING GAOL AND OTHER POEMS, Oscar Wilde. 64pp. 27072-6 $1.00

EARLY POEMS, William Carlos Williams. 64pp. (Available in U.S. only.) 29294-0 $1.00

FAVORITE POEMS, William Wordsworth. 80pp. 27073-4 $1.00

WORLD WAR ONE BRITISH POETS: Brooke, Owen, Sassoon, Rosenberg, and Others, Candace Ward (ed.). (Available in U.S. only.) 29568-0 $1.00

EARLY POEMS, William Butler Yeats. 128pp. 27808-5 $1.50

"EASTER, 1916" AND OTHER POEMS, William Butler Yeats. 80pp. (Available in U.S. only.) 29771-3 $1.00

DOVER · THRIFT · EDITIONS

FICTION

FLATLAND: A ROMANCE OF MANY DIMENSIONS, Edwin A. Abbott. 96pp. 27263-X $1.00

SHORT STORIES, Louisa May Alcott. 64pp. 29063-8 $1.00

WINESBURG, OHIO, Sherwood Anderson. 160pp. 28269-4 $2.00

PERSUASION, Jane Austen. 224pp. 29555-9 $2.00

PRIDE AND PREJUDICE, Jane Austen. 272pp. 28473-5 $2.00

SENSE AND SENSIBILITY, Jane Austen. 272pp. 29049-2 $2.00

LOOKING BACKWARD, Edward Bellamy. 160pp. 29038-7 $2.00

BEOWULF, Beowulf (trans. by R. K. Gordon). 64pp. 27264-8 $1.00

CIVIL WAR STORIES, Ambrose Bierce. 128pp. 28038-1 $1.00

"THE MOONLIT ROAD" AND OTHER GHOST AND HORROR STORIES, Ambrose Bierce (John Grafton, ed.) 96pp. 40056-5 $1.00

WUTHERING HEIGHTS, Emily Brontë. 256pp. 29256-8 $2.00

THE THIRTY-NINE STEPS, John Buchan. 96pp. 28201-5 $1.50

TARZAN OF THE APES, Edgar Rice Burroughs. 224pp. (Available in U.S. only.) 29570-2 $2.00

ALICE'S ADVENTURES IN WONDERLAND, Lewis Carroll. 96pp. 27543-4 $1.00

THROUGH THE LOOKING-GLASS, Lewis Carroll. 128pp. 40878-7 $1.50

MY ÁNTONIA, Willa Cather. 176pp. 28240-6 $2.00

O PIONEERS!, Willa Cather. 128pp. 27785-2 $1.00

PAUL'S CASE AND OTHER STORIES, Willa Cather. 64pp. 29057-3 $1.00

FIVE GREAT SHORT STORIES, Anton Chekhov. 96pp. 26463-7 $1.00

TALES OF CONJURE AND THE COLOR LINE, Charles Waddell Chesnutt. 128pp. 40426-9 $1.50

FAVORITE FATHER BROWN STORIES, G. K. Chesterton. 96pp. 27545-0 $1.00

THE AWAKENING, Kate Chopin. 128pp. 27786-0 $1.00

A PAIR OF SILK STOCKINGS AND OTHER STORIES, Kate Chopin. 64pp. 29264-9 $1.00

HEART OF DARKNESS, Joseph Conrad. 80pp. 26464-5 $1.00

LORD JIM, Joseph Conrad. 256pp. 40650-4 $2.00

THE SECRET SHARER AND OTHER STORIES, Joseph Conrad. 128pp. 27546-9 $1.00

THE "LITTLE REGIMENT" AND OTHER CIVIL WAR STORIES, Stephen Crane. 80pp. 29557-5 $1.00

THE OPEN BOAT AND OTHER STORIES, Stephen Crane. 128pp. 27547-7 $1.50

THE RED BADGE OF COURAGE, Stephen Crane. 112pp. 26465-3 $1.00

MOLL FLANDERS, Daniel Defoe. 256pp. 29093-X $2.00

ROBINSON CRUSOE, Daniel Defoe. 288pp. 40427-7 $2.00

A CHRISTMAS CAROL, Charles Dickens. 80pp. 26865-9 $1.00

THE CRICKET ON THE HEARTH AND OTHER CHRISTMAS STORIES, Charles Dickens. 128pp. 28039-X $1.00

A TALE OF TWO CITIES, Charles Dickens. 304pp. 40651-2 $2.00

THE DOUBLE, Fyodor Dostoyevsky. 128pp. 29572-9 $1.50

THE GAMBLER, Fyodor Dostoyevsky. 112pp. 29081-6 $1.50

NOTES FROM THE UNDERGROUND, Fyodor Dostoyevsky. 96pp. 27053-X $1.00

THE ADVENTURE OF THE DANCING MEN AND OTHER STORIES, Sir Arthur Conan Doyle. 80pp. 29558-3 $1.00

THE HOUND OF THE BASKERVILLES, Arthur Conan Doyle. 128pp. 28214-7 $1.50

THE LOST WORLD, Arthur Conan Doyle. 176pp. 40060-3 $1.50

DOVER · THRIFT · EDITIONS

FICTION

SIX GREAT SHERLOCK HOLMES STORIES, Sir Arthur Conan Doyle. 112pp. 27055-6 $1.00

SILAS MARNER, George Eliot. 160pp. 29246-0 $1.50

THIS SIDE OF PARADISE, F. Scott Fitzgerald. 208pp. 28999-0 $2.00

"THE DIAMOND AS BIG AS THE RITZ" AND OTHER STORIES, F. Scott Fitzgerald. 29991-0 $2.00

THE REVOLT OF "MOTHER" AND OTHER STORIES, Mary E. Wilkins Freeman. 128pp. 40428-5 $1.50

MADAME BOVARY, Gustave Flaubert. 256pp. 29257-6 $2.00

WHERE ANGELS FEAR TO TREAD, E. M. Forster. 128pp. (Available in U.S. only.) 27791-7 $1.50

A ROOM WITH A VIEW, E. M. Forster. 176pp. (Available in U.S. only.) 28467-0 $2.00

THE IMMORALIST, André Gide. 112pp. (Available in U.S. only.) 29237-1 $1.50

"THE YELLOW WALLPAPER" AND OTHER STORIES, Charlotte Perkins Gilman. 80pp. 29857-4 $1.00

HERLAND, Charlotte Perkins Gilman. 128pp. 40429-3 $1.50

THE OVERCOAT AND OTHER STORIES, Nikolai Gogol. 112pp. 27057-2 $1.50

GREAT GHOST STORIES, John Grafton (ed.). 112pp. 27270-2 $1.00

DETECTION BY GASLIGHT, Douglas G. Greene (ed.). 272pp. 29928-7 $2.00

THE MABINOGION, Lady Charlotte E. Guest. 192pp. 29541-9 $2.00

"THE FIDDLER OF THE REELS" AND OTHER SHORT STORIES, Thomas Hardy. 80pp. 29960-0 $1.50

THE LUCK OF ROARING CAMP AND OTHER STORIES, Bret Harte. 96pp. 27271-0 $1.00

THE SCARLET LETTER, Nathaniel Hawthorne. 192pp. 28048-9 $2.00

YOUNG GOODMAN BROWN AND OTHER STORIES, Nathaniel Hawthorne. 128pp. 27060-2 $1.00

THE GIFT OF THE MAGI AND OTHER SHORT STORIES, O. Henry. 96pp. 27061-0 $1.00

THE NUTCRACKER AND THE GOLDEN POT, E. T. A. Hoffmann. 128pp. 27806-9 $1.00

THE BEAST IN THE JUNGLE AND OTHER STORIES, Henry James. 128pp. 27552-3 $1.50

DAISY MILLER, Henry James. 64pp. 28773-4 $1.00

THE TURN OF THE SCREW, Henry James. 96pp. 26684-2 $1.00

WASHINGTON SQUARE, Henry James. 176pp. 40431-5 $2.00

THE COUNTRY OF THE POINTED FIRS, Sarah Orne Jewett. 96pp. 28196-5 $1.00

THE AUTOBIOGRAPHY OF AN EX-COLORED MAN, James Weldon Johnson. 112pp. 28512-X $1.00

DUBLINERS, James Joyce. 160pp. 26870-5 $1.00

A PORTRAIT OF THE ARTIST AS A YOUNG MAN, James Joyce. 192pp. 28050-0 $2.00

THE METAMORPHOSIS AND OTHER STORIES, Franz Kafka. 96pp. 29030-1 $1.50

THE MAN WHO WOULD BE KING AND OTHER STORIES, Rudyard Kipling. 128pp. 28051-9 $1.50

YOU KNOW ME AL, Ring Lardner. 128pp. 28513-8 $1.50

SELECTED SHORT STORIES, D. H. Lawrence. 128pp. 27794-1 $1.50

GREEN TEA AND OTHER GHOST STORIES, J. Sheridan LeFanu. 96pp. 27795-X $1.50

SHORT STORIES, Theodore Dreiser. 112pp. 28215-5 $1.50

THE CALL OF THE WILD, Jack London. 64pp. 26472-6 $1.00

FIVE GREAT SHORT STORIES, Jack London. 96pp. 27063-7 $1.00

WHITE FANG, Jack London. 160pp. 26968-X $1.00

DEATH IN VENICE, Thomas Mann. 96pp. (Available in U.S. only.) 28714-9 $1.00

IN A GERMAN PENSION: 13 Stories, Katherine Mansfield. 112pp. 28719-X $1.50

THE MOON AND SIXPENCE, W. Somerset Maugham. 176pp. (Available in U.S. only.) 28731-9 $2.00

DOVER·THRIFT·EDITIONS

FICTION

THE NECKLACE AND OTHER SHORT STORIES, Guy de Maupassant. 128pp. 27064-5 $1.00

BARTLEBY AND BENITO CERENO, Herman Melville. 112pp. 26473-4 $1.00

THE OIL JAR AND OTHER STORIES, Luigi Pirandello. 96pp. 28459-X $1.00

THE GOLD-BUG AND OTHER TALES, Edgar Allan Poe. 128pp. 26875-6 $1.00

TALES OF TERROR AND DETECTION, Edgar Allan Poe. 96pp. 28744-0 $1.00

THE QUEEN OF SPADES AND OTHER STORIES, Alexander Pushkin. 128pp. 28054-3 $1.50

SREDNI VASHTAR AND OTHER STORIES, Saki (H. H. Munro). 96pp. 28521-9 $1.00

THE STORY OF AN AFRICAN FARM, Olive Schreiner. 256pp. 40165-0 $2.00

FRANKENSTEIN, Mary Shelley. 176pp. 28211-2 $1.00

THREE LIVES, Gertrude Stein. 176pp. (Available in U.S. only.) 28059-4 $2.00

THE STRANGE CASE OF DR. JEKYLL AND MR. HYDE, Robert Louis Stevenson. 64pp. 26688-5 $1.00

TREASURE ISLAND, Robert Louis Stevenson. 160pp. 27559-0 $1.50

GULLIVER'S TRAVELS, Jonathan Swift. 240pp. 29273-8 $2.00

THE KREUTZER SONATA AND OTHER SHORT STORIES, Leo Tolstoy. 144pp. 27805-0 $1.50

THE WARDEN, Anthony Trollope. 176pp. 40076-X $2.00

FIRST LOVE AND DIARY OF A SUPERFLUOUS MAN, Ivan Turgenev. 96pp. 28775-0 $1.50

FATHERS AND SONS, Ivan Turgenev. 176pp. 40073-5 $2.00

ADVENTURES OF HUCKLEBERRY FINN, Mark Twain. 224pp. 28061-6 $2.00

THE ADVENTURES OF TOM SAWYER, Mark Twain. 192pp. 40077-8 $2.00

THE MYSTERIOUS STRANGER AND OTHER STORIES, Mark Twain. 128pp. 27069-6 $1.00

HUMOROUS STORIES AND SKETCHES, Mark Twain. 80pp. 29279-7 $1.00

CANDIDE, Voltaire (François-Marie Arouet). 112pp. 26689-3 $1.00

GREAT SHORT STORIES BY AMERICAN WOMEN, Candace Ward (ed.). 192pp. 28776-9 $2.00

"THE COUNTRY OF THE BLIND" AND OTHER SCIENCE-FICTION STORIES, H. G. Wells. 160pp. (Available in U.S. only.) 29569-9 $1.00

THE ISLAND OF DR. MOREAU, H. G. Wells. 112pp. (Available in U.S. only.) 29027-1 $1.50

THE INVISIBLE MAN, H. G. Wells. 112pp. (Available in U.S. only.) 27071-8 $1.00

THE TIME MACHINE, H. G. Wells. 80pp. (Available in U.S. only.) 28472-7 $1.00

THE WAR OF THE WORLDS, H. G. Wells. 160pp. (Available in U.S. only.) 29506-0 $1.00

ETHAN FROME, Edith Wharton. 96pp. 26690-7 $1.00

SHORT STORIES, Edith Wharton. 128pp. 28235-X $1.50

THE AGE OF INNOCENCE, Edith Wharton. 288pp. 29803-5 $2.00

THE PICTURE OF DORIAN GRAY, Oscar Wilde. 192pp. 27807-7 $1.50

JACOB'S ROOM, Virginia Woolf. 144pp. (Available in U.S. only.) 40109-X $1.50

MONDAY OR TUESDAY: Eight Stories, Virginia Woolf. 64pp. (Available in U.S. only.) 29453-6 $1.00

NONFICTION

POETICS, Aristotle. 64pp. 29577-X $1.00

NICOMACHEAN ETHICS, Aristotle. 256pp. 40096-4 $2.00

MEDITATIONS, Marcus Aurelius. 128pp. 29823-X $1.50

THE LAND OF LITTLE RAIN, Mary Austin. 96pp. 29037-9 $1.50

THE DEVIL'S DICTIONARY, Ambrose Bierce. 144pp. 27542-6 $1.00

THE ANALECTS, Confucius. 128pp. 28484-0 $2.00

CONFESSIONS OF AN ENGLISH OPIUM EATER, Thomas De Quincey. 80pp. 28742-4 $1.00

NARRATIVE OF THE LIFE OF FREDERICK DOUGLASS, Frederick Douglass. 96pp. 28499-9 $1.00

DOVER · THRIFT · EDITIONS

NONFICTION

THE SOULS OF BLACK FOLK, W. E. B. Du Bois. 176pp. 28041-1 $2.00

SELF-RELIANCE AND OTHER ESSAYS, Ralph Waldo Emerson. 128pp. 27790-9 $1.00

THE LIFE OF OLAUDAH EQUIANO, OR GUSTAVUS VASSA, THE AFRICAN, Olaudah Equiano. 192pp. 40661-X $2.00

THE AUTOBIOGRAPHY OF BENJAMIN FRANKLIN, Benjamin Franklin. 144pp. 29073-5 $1.50

TOTEM AND TABOO, Sigmund Freud. 176pp. (Available in U.S. only.) 40434-X $2.00

LOVE: A Book of Quotations, Herb Galewitz (ed.). 64pp. 40004-2 $1.00

PRAGMATISM, William James. 128pp. 28270-8 $1.50

THE STORY OF MY LIFE, Helen Keller. 80pp. 29249-5 $1.00

TAO TE CHING, Lao Tze. 112pp. 29792-6 $1.00

GREAT SPEECHES, Abraham Lincoln. 112pp. 26872-1 $1.00

THE PRINCE, Niccolò Machiavelli. 80pp. 27274-5 $1.00

THE SUBJECTION OF WOMEN, John Stuart Mill. 112pp. 29601-6 $1.50

SELECTED ESSAYS, Michel de Montaigne. 96pp. 29109-X $1.50

UTOPIA, Sir Thomas More. 96pp. 29583-4 $1.50

BEYOND GOOD AND EVIL: Prelude to a Philosophy of the Future, Friedrich Nietzsche. 176pp. 29868-X $1.50

THE BIRTH OF TRAGEDY, Friedrich Nietzsche. 96pp. 28515-4 $1.50

COMMON SENSE, Thomas Paine. 64pp. 29602-4 $1.00

SYMPOSIUM AND PHAEDRUS, Plato. 96pp. 27798-4 $1.50

THE TRIAL AND DEATH OF SOCRATES: Four Dialogues, Plato. 128pp. 27066-1 $1.00

A MODEST PROPOSAL AND OTHER SATIRICAL WORKS, Jonathan Swift. 64pp. 28759-9 $1.00

CIVIL DISOBEDIENCE AND OTHER ESSAYS, Henry David Thoreau. 96pp. 27563-9 $1.00

SELECTIONS FROM THE JOURNALS (Edited by Walter Harding), Henry David Thoreau. 96pp. 28760-2 $1.00

WALDEN; OR, LIFE IN THE WOODS, Henry David Thoreau. 224pp. 28495-6 $2.00

NARRATIVE OF SOJOURNER TRUTH, Sojourner Truth. 80pp. 29899-X $1.00

THE THEORY OF THE LEISURE CLASS, Thorstein Veblen. 256pp. 28062-4 $2.50

DE PROFUNDIS, Oscar Wilde. 64pp. 29308-4 $1.00

OSCAR WILDE'S WIT AND WISDOM: A Book of Quotations, Oscar Wilde. 64pp. 40146-4 $1.00

UP FROM SLAVERY, Booker T. Washington. 160pp. 28738-6 $2.00

A VINDICATION OF THE RIGHTS OF WOMAN, Mary Wollstonecraft. 224pp. 29036-0 $2.00

PLAYS

PROMETHEUS BOUND, Aeschylus. 64pp. 28762-9 $1.00

THE ORESTEIA TRILOGY: Agamemnon, The Libation-Bearers and The Furies, Aeschylus. 160pp. 29242-8 $1.50

LYSISTRATA, Aristophanes. 64pp. 28225-2 $1.00

WHAT EVERY WOMAN KNOWS, James Barrie. 80pp. (Available in U.S. only.) 29578-8 $1.50

THE CHERRY ORCHARD, Anton Chekhov. 64pp. 26682-6 $1.00

THE SEA GULL, Anton Chekhov. 64pp. 40656-3 $1.50

THE THREE SISTERS, Anton Chekhov. 64pp. 27544-2 $1.50

UNCLE VANYA, Anton Chekhov. 64pp. 40159-6 $1.50

THE WAY OF THE WORLD, William Congreve. 80pp. 27787-9 $1.50

BACCHAE, Euripides. 64pp. 29580-X $1.00

MEDEA, Euripides. 64pp. 27548-5 $1.00

THE MIKADO, William Schwenck Gilbert. 64pp. 27268-0 $1.50

DOVER·THRIFT·EDITIONS

PLAYS

FAUST, PART ONE, Johann Wolfgang von Goethe. 192pp. 28046-2 $2.00
THE INSPECTOR GENERAL, Nikolai Gogol. 80pp. 28500-6 $1.50
SHE STOOPS TO CONQUER, Oliver Goldsmith. 80pp. 26867-5 $1.50
A DOLL'S HOUSE, Henrik Ibsen. 80pp. 27062-9 $1.00
GHOSTS, Henrik Ibsen. 64pp. 29852-3 $1.50
HEDDA GABLER, Henrik Ibsen. 80pp. 26469-6 $1.50
THE WILD DUCK, Henrik Ibsen. 96pp. 41116-8 $1.50
VOLPONE, Ben Jonson. 112pp. 28049-7 $1.50
DR. FAUSTUS, Christopher Marlowe. 64pp. 28208-2 $1.50
THE MISANTHROPE, Molière. 64pp. 27065-3 $1.00
ANNA CHRISTIE, Eugene O'Neill. 80pp. 29985-6 $1.50
BEYOND THE HORIZON, Eugene O'Neill. 96pp. 29085-9 $1.50
THE EMPEROR JONES, Eugene O'Neill. 64pp. 29268-1 $1.50
THE LONG VOYAGE HOME AND OTHER PLAYS, Eugene O'Neill. 80pp. 28755-6 $1.50
RIGHT YOU ARE, IF YOU THINK YOU ARE, Luigi Pirandello. 64pp. (Available in U.S. only.)
  29576-1 $1.50
SIX CHARACTERS IN SEARCH OF AN AUTHOR, Luigi Pirandello. 64pp. (Available in U.S. only.)
  29992-9 $1.50
HANDS AROUND, Arthur Schnitzler. 64pp. 28724-6 $1.00
ANTONY AND CLEOPATRA, William Shakespeare. 128pp. 40062-X $1.50
AS YOU LIKE IT, William Shakespeare. 80pp. 40432-3 $1.50
HAMLET, William Shakespeare. 128pp. 27278-8 $1.00
HENRY IV, William Shakespeare. 96pp. 29584-2 $1.00
JULIUS CAESAR, William Shakespeare. 80pp. 26876-4 $1.00
KING LEAR, William Shakespeare. 112pp. 28058-6 $1.00
MACBETH, William Shakespeare. 96pp. 27802-6 $1.00
MEASURE FOR MEASURE, William Shakespeare. 96pp. 40889-2 $1.50
THE MERCHANT OF VENICE, William Shakespeare. 96pp. 28492-1 $1.00
A MIDSUMMER NIGHT'S DREAM, William Shakespeare. 80pp. 27067-X $1.00
MUCH ADO ABOUT NOTHING, William Shakespeare. 80pp. 28272-4 $1.00
OTHELLO, William Shakespeare. 112pp. 29097-2 $1.00
RICHARD III, William Shakespeare. 112pp. 28747-5 $1.00
ROMEO AND JULIET, William Shakespeare. 96pp. 27557-4 $1.00
THE TAMING OF THE SHREW, William Shakespeare. 96pp. 29765-9 $1.00
THE TEMPEST, William Shakespeare. 96pp. 40658-X $1.50
TWELFTH NIGHT; OR, WHAT YOU WILL, William Shakespeare. 80pp. 29290-8 $1.00
ARMS AND THE MAN, George Bernard Shaw. 80pp. (Available in U.S. only.) 26476-9 $1.50
HEARTBREAK HOUSE, George Bernard Shaw. 128pp. (Available in U.S. only.) 29291-6 $1.50
PYGMALION, George Bernard Shaw. 96pp. (Available in U.S. only.) 28222-8 $1.00
THE RIVALS, Richard Brinsley Sheridan. 96pp. 40433-1 $1.50
THE SCHOOL FOR SCANDAL, Richard Brinsley Sheridan. 96pp. 26687-7 $1.50
ANTIGONE, Sophocles. 64pp. 27804-2 $1.00
OEDIPUS AT COLONUS, Sophocles. 64pp. 40659-8 $1.00
OEDIPUS REX, Sophocles. 64pp. 26877-2 $1.00
ELECTRA, Sophocles. 64pp. 28482-4 $1.00
MISS JULIE, August Strindberg. 64pp. 27281-8 $1.50
THE PLAYBOY OF THE WESTERN WORLD AND RIDERS TO THE SEA, J. M. Synge. 80pp.
  27562-0 $1.50
THE DUCHESS OF MALFI, John Webster. 96pp. 40660-1 $1.00
THE IMPORTANCE OF BEING EARNEST, Oscar Wilde. 64pp. 26478-5 $1.00
LADY WINDERMERE'S FAN, Oscar Wilde. 64pp. 40078-6 $1.00